The Anxiety Sufferer's Tool Book

Maria Albertsen

with Jan Albertsen

© 2013 Maria Albertsen

It is the right of Maria Albertsen to be identified as the author of this work. This right is asserted world-wide. All rights reserved. No part of this publication may be produced, stored or transmitted in any form by any means, including; electrical, mechanical or otherwise without the prior written consent of the author.

The author, publishers and their representatives cannot be held responsible for any error in detail, accuracy or judgment whatsoever. The Anxiety Sufferer's Tool Book is sold on this understanding.

ISBN: 1482609398

ISBN-13: 978-1482609394

Graphics and Images by Maria Albertsen.

Cover photo by Matthew Butcher and Oliver Robertson.

Disclaimer

Please note that while the 'tools' in this book can help a multitude of problems, they are not intended to be used as a replacement for medical treatment, but can usually be used in conjunction with it. Please discuss these issues with your therapist or doctor. When you use these techniques on yourself, you are taking full responsibility for your physical and emotional wellbeing. Please exercise common sense on the issues you choose to work with and contact relevant practitioners if you need further advice. Your GP should be able to make any necessary referrals. The authors or anyone associated with this book cannot be held responsible for any of your actions or your well-being, either physically, mentally, emotional or otherwise as a result of using the 'tools' in this book. The aim of the information in this book is to give you an idea of how it can be used to heal your anxiety. We do not claim to be partaking in any therapeutic work with you, more giving you the information you need to heal yourself.

Please note that the links to our website throughout this book may expire or change over time. Please ensure you visit these links to print out relevant material if you wish to do so. We cannot be held accountable for links that change or expire over time. If you find a link is not working then please contact us as we will usually be able to provide you with the relevant information.

CONTENTS

A word from the Author	Page 1
Introduction	4
So what is anxiety?	6
Tool 1 – Identifying triggers, challenging self and making changes	10
Tool 2 – Affirmations	17
Tool 3 – Focused breathing	22
Tool 4 – Emotional Freedom Technique (EFT)	28
Tool 5 – Distraction methods	35
Tool 6 – Self care - Self-massage, diet and exercise	38
Tool 7 – Diary and journal writing	57
Tool 8 – Visualisation for mind relaxation	63
Tool 9 – Physical relaxation	67
Tool 10 - Unwanted Thoughts – The stop, rewind and re-play method	72
Conclusion	76
About the authors	78
Connect with us	79

READER REVIEWS

"What a fantastic book! I found this really helpful, will definitely recommend to others I know who suffer anxiety. Well worth the wait!" ~ S Jones

"I have to say I think it is really good. You explain more about the solutions rather than the problem and I find that so incredibly positive. I love the EFT section and I have been using this at night (this is when I suffer dreadfully)." ~ E Furness

"It's inspirational...it's not full of the whole "body needs this and that blah blah blah". You got straight to the point." ~ D Rochford

"My name is Michelle and I have spent 10 years and 8 attempts at passing my driving test. My problem with the test was nerves, I could drive fine, but put me in a car with an examiner and my brain went to mush! My 8th attempt at my driving test I knew needed to be my last and final attempt as I could not keep putting myself through the stress of it. I had tried everything in the past to calm myself before the test, I had even got beta blockers from the doctor for one of them! I had discussed with Maria my whole phobia of driving tests and literally 2 days before my test Maria suggested to me had I tried the EFT technique? I had never heard of this before and when I read it, I honestly did think that there was no chance it would work! However I was desperate to give anything a go and I did try this and I was immediately surprised at how much of a calming effect it had on me. I only used the technique a few times before my actual test and then I did it in the waiting room before the test. I've never been so calm and concentrated before a test. This time I finally passed my test and I am so grateful to Maria for introducing me to the EFT technique as I feel it really did pay off for me!" ~ Michelle

"I found this book really helpful. It was written in a clear way, with none of the 'fussiness' that I feel most similar books have. Understanding that everyone deals with their anxiety in a different way, there were several techniques explained. I would definitely recommend this book to anyone suffering with anxiety." ~ L, Gordon

MARIA ALBERTSEN

ACKNOWLEDGMENTS

I would like to thank the many clients who have spent time with me over the years and have worked with me to practice some old and develop some new techniques for anxiety relief. I would also like to thank an old counsellor of mine who helped me to overcome my own anxiety and started me on my journey to help and support others, you know who you are!

Of course, a huge thanks to my wonderful husband Jan, who has contributed to this book and helped make it what it is today. Thank you Jan.

I would also like to thank my Mam and little sister Debbie, for letting me take photos of them and use them throughout this book.

A special thanks goes to Matthew and Oliver who took the beautiful picture on the front cover and allowed me to use it. Matt has provided us with the following words about the actual photograph.

"This was taken at sunrise on a volcano called Kelimutu in Flores. Flores is an island belonging to Indonesia. Oli and I climbed to the crater lakes and watched the sunrise with about another 15 people. There were also some locals selling ginger coffee and so we sat and watched the sunrise whilst sipping coffee. There were also some naughty monkeys playing around us and trying to get some scraps of food if anyone had anything. It was so peaceful and as you can see just stunning, the picture doesn't do it justice (although not far off)."

I'm sure everyone will agree it is a stunning scene.

With love

Maria

A WORD FROM THE AUTHOR

Hi there and thank you for purchasing this book, you've taken the first step towards becoming anxiety free. What I want to share with you is the ability to;

> **"recognise and overcome anxiety symptoms for life..."**

Now why should you believe what I say?

Anxiety has been in my life for a long time, first as a sufferer and secondly as a qualified counsellor and psychotherapist where I have worked with many people to help them overcome anxiety. I suffered from anxiety and panic attacks for about 8 years and it was only with the help of a counsellor that I learned the 'tools' to use to overcome them. At one point my anxiety was so bad that I could not even think about leaving the house without being sick! So I do understand what it really is like to have anxiety that controls your life.

In 2005 I qualified as a counsellor and became accredited with the BACP (British Association of Counselling and Psychotherapy). During my counselling practice I used the same tools that I am about to share with you in this book. I stopped practicing as a counsellor in 2011 and put my BACP membership on hold as I wanted to focus on raising my two sons, age 3 and 4 years. However, one day I was looking at all the books out there about anxiety and they all seemed like very long reads and a lot of them, in my opinion, tend to over analyse things. What I always found throughout my work as a counsellor was that people didn't want to analyse what was wrong with them, they just wanted to feel better, and so that is the aim of this book, to help you feel better!

I feel very passionate about this subject and it is my hope that this book will give you the tools you need to help you to recognise and overcome the anxiety you are experiencing, forever. This may sound like a big claim to you, but remember these tools have been practiced and proven to work. The trick is that you need to follow them with commitment to ensure they work for you too. I believe that the tools in this book will also help to stop panic attacks and deal with stress, depression and OCD (obsessive compulsive disorder) as well as a range of other emotional issues too.

You need to enter into this book with an open mind. Some of the tools I am about to show you may seem a little strange and perhaps even silly, but they do work and can work for you too. They don't need to be over thought or over analysed, just a simple belief and trust that they will work should do the trick. They need to be practiced more than once, usually once a day for a few days before you will start to notice any difference. A lot of people often try something once or twice and say that it does not work and so give up. This is sad as if they just persevere for a week or so then I know one or more of these tools will start to make a real difference to their life.

This book will help you to recognise what is triggering your anxiety and will then show you how you can learn to cope with or get rid of it completely. By trying out all of these tools you can then choose what works best for you.

What I often used to encounter when I counselled people with anxiety was that they felt a certain degree of unfairness, often asking why they had anxiety and not someone else or what they had done to deserve this. There is no simple answer to this and one of the awful things about life is that we have to deal with feelings that are not there as a result of something we have done, but are there simply because they are. Yes, it is horrible that we have to deal with this and it can feel like hard work at times, but at the end of the day there is a choice you need to make. Do you want to go through life day to day scared about how you are feeling and dreading an anxiety attack? Or do you want to put a little hard work and effort in for the short term and learn the tools I am about to show you that will mean you can banish anxiety from your life, and have the means and knowledge to cope with it should it arise again? If you choose the latter, then welcome! You've just achieved the second step and that is choosing to do something about it. You can choose to live your life anxiety free and this book can help you do just that. If you are still not sure then why not give it a go anyway, what have you got to lose?

So what are we waiting for, let's get this journey started.

Maria

p.s. If you have any questions and would like to contact me, details are provided at the end of this book.

INTRODUCTION

Before you begin to read this book I want you to do one important thing first. I want you to get a piece of paper, just a little bit and write on it, 'I will be ok'. Now you may think this is funny, perhaps a little strange even, but we will learn more about this later in the book. What I want you to do each day, until you get to the part in the book where I tell you to stop, is to keep this piece of paper in your pocket wherever you go and each morning say to yourself, "I will be ok". You should repeat this 10 times. You can either say it in your head or out loud, that's up to you. Then do the same at night just before you go to bed. Each time you say it hold the piece of paper in your hand.

What you'll find in the chapters throughout this book are tools you can use to control anxiety and even banish it from your life forever. Throughout my work as a counsellor, with hundreds of clients with this problem, they have proven to be effective time and time again. I believe that if you put them into practice in the way I say and stick with them then you too will learn to deal with your own anxiety. I really believe that with a little hard work, you can become anxiety free!

What can you expect from this book?

I do not believe you would have sought out a book as focused as this one if you were not experiencing anxiety and looking to overcome it.

This tells me that you probably already know what anxiety is. For me personally, and from my work with clients, I have found that anxiety sufferers usually do not want a lot of information about anxiety as such. They just want rid of it! As part of overcoming anxiety we do need to have a little understanding about it which is why I have included the next chapter, which you will notice is very brief. I tend to like to be proactive in my work, and my aim with this book is to reflect this and to focus more on the tools you can use to overcome anxiety as effectively and quickly as possible.

You will also notice that I have brought in some expert help from a qualified counsellor, psychotherapist, EFT (Level 2) practitioner and clinical hypnotherapist (who just happens to be my husband!) to work with me to ensure you are receiving the best possible and up to date information that we can provide you with.

Throughout the book there are examples of worksheets. For your convenience I have added these to our website and have included the links you can use to download the sheets throughout the book. You may print these out for personal use only.

SO WHAT IS ANXIETY?

If you can relate to some of the symptoms below then you are probably experiencing some level of anxiety which is affecting your life.

Signs and symptoms of an anxiety disorder.

* You avoid things that make you anxious.
* You feel constantly tense, worried, or on edge.
* Anxiety interferes with your work, school, family and/or social life.
* You have irrational fears, thoughts and/or feelings that you can't seem to control.
* You believe bad things are going to happen.

Physical symptoms of anxiety.

* Dizziness.
* Your heart starts pounding.
* You start sweating.
* You have stomach upset, vomiting or diarrhea.
* Frequent urination.
* Shortness of breath.
* Tremors and twitches.
* Muscle tension.
* Headaches.

* Fatigue.

Emotional symptoms of anxiety.

* Feelings of apprehension or dread.
* Difficulty concentrating or making decisions.
* Feeling tense, shaky and jumpy.
* Anticipating the worst, believing it will happen.
* Irritability.
* Restlessness.
* Feeling like your mind's gone blank, distant from reality.

Is there a difference between anxiety and an anxiety attack?

Anxiety can be a very scary and difficult thing to deal with. Anyone who has experienced the symptoms above will probably tell you it is one of the hardest things they have ever had to deal with, and it has stopped them from living the life they wanted to.

Anxiety can vary from person to person, for some it may be nothing more than 'normal' anxiety where they get the expected nerves about giving a speech or sitting a driving test for example. For others, anxiety can happen for no apparent reason and can often be debilitating, some people may not even feel they can leave their home.

I believe that anxiety can be described as those uneasy, scary, tense, and worried or on edge feelings we get or those unwanted thoughts that make us feel that way. If you are anxious you may avoid things that make you feel this way or you may feel anxious for some unknown reason too. These feelings can come and go or may seem like they are there for most of the time. An anxiety attack is usually more severe, and accompanied by the more scary physical symptoms such as shortness of breath, heart pounding, sweating, trembling and vomiting and those more severe feelings where a person really believes they are going to die. The tools in this book can help both sufferers of anxiety and anxiety attacks. You can practice them when you are feeling okay, anxious or having an actual attack. I personally use a lot of Emotional Freedom Techniques (EFT), as shown in Tool 4. EFT works especially for me if I am ever feeling like I am on the edge of having an anxiety/panic attack; it stops it from actually happening. This technique has changed my life. It has helped me to cope with various stressful situations such as when my son was admitted to hospital and I was very anxious, it calmed me down and I was more able to be there for him.

To summarise, I usually say anxiety is a problem if it stops you from living your life and stops you from doing the things you'd like to do.

My aim is not to give you a book which is a big read about what anxiety is and why we have it, but I just think it is important to mention the following fact before we move on to look at the tools in this book that you can put into practice.

Anxiety is a normal bodily function. It is part of our 'flight' or 'fight' response which all animals have and acts as a way to protect ourselves. For example, if you are walking down a street and all is quiet and well you will probably feel quite calm and okay with your surroundings. However, if a big dog jumped out at you and started barking you would probably experience some of the anxiety symptoms listed above. This is because your body has reacted to protect you. It is telling you to either stay and 'fight' or run away 'flight', whichever you choose your body produces adrenaline and other chemicals to facilitate this process. Now this is helpful in many situations where we need to act quickly to protect ourselves and others, but it is very scary when it happens for no apparent reason, which is the case for a lot of anxiety sufferers. I am not going to get into the details, like a lot of anxiety books out there do, about how this process has evolved over time, or how our parasympathetic nervous system works or how cardiovascular activation by the sympathetic nervous system works, because most people who I have worked with have no desire to understand these processes. They just want rid of their anxiety!

Now I know you may have heard about the 'fight or flight' response before but I just think it is a good way of re-affirming to yourself that you are 'normal', because you have anxiety does not mean you are, 'mad' or 'stupid' or 'weak' or 'over-sensitive' or anything else you may have told yourself or have been told by others.

Okay, now that that's clear I'd like to move onto the exciting part, and I do hope you find it exciting as I fully believe that you do not have to let anxiety control your life, **YOU CAN CONTROL IT!**

THE ANXIETY SUFFERER'S TOOL BOOK

**"You do not have to let anxiety control your life.
You can control it".**

So, are you ready? Yes? Well than let's read the book and get on with it! No? Let's read the book and get on with it anyway!

You will be anxiety free.

Tool 1
Identifying triggers, challenging self and making changes

Identifying triggers

What I can guarantee, even if you are not aware of it yet, is that there will be certain events or situations in your life that cause you to feel anxious. These events and situations are called 'triggers' and by recognising what they are you can take steps to overcome the anxiety associated with them. For example, whenever I felt anxious I really believed I had no idea why this was and thought that there must be something wrong with me. Then I had an idea and thought that if I kept a log of my week and highlighted the times I felt anxious that maybe I would learn from this. And guess what....I did! It has worked for many clients too.

Now I'm going to show you how to use the same daily log which will highlight anything that triggers your anxiety. On the next page is an example of a daily log sheet you can use to fill in throughout your week. Where you see in the box to give a score, this should be a score out of 10, with 1 being, 'I didn't feel anxious at all' to 10 being, 'I felt the most anxious I could ever feel'. Only fill in each table at the end of each day and then answer the questions below the table. You should have 7 sheets at the end of the week (one for each day). I have filled in one line of the table and answered the questions below it to show you how it can be used. At the end of the week you will be able to see a pattern of any events, activities or tasks that cause you to feel anxious and any people associated with them. Once you identify these patterns you can then take the necessary steps to change them, which we will look at shortly.

Example

Day: Monday   **Date:** 1st Oct

Event/activity/task (E/A/T)	Time	Score how anxious you felt before the E/A/T	Who was present?	Score how anxious you felt during the E/A/T	Score how anxious you felt after the E/A/T
Lunch time at work	12pm	8	Work mates	7	2

Q1. What were you thinking throughout each E/A/T?

    A. I'm slightly overweight and was thinking that my work mates would think I shouldn't be eating and should be on a diet. I thought about the possibility of going to lunch alone.

Q2. What were you feeling throughout each E/A/T?

    A. I was feeling self-conscious and paranoid. I feel fat since I had my second baby and feel like it's a struggle to lose any weight.

Q3. Go through each E/A/T and highlight anything that appears again and again in the different columns for each E/A/T?

    A. * Use this space to look for patterns; in this case it would be to see if I felt paranoid or self-conscious when eating around other people too. Did I feel this way at lunch time every day at work? Or was it just when I took my break with certain individuals? This will enable you to identify if the same people are present when you feel anxious.

Q4. What patterns do you notice?

    A. I notice that I feel paranoid around people who I think are slimmer and better looking than me. I feel like they are judging me. I feel ok when I am eating with family as I know they don't judge me. They are aware of how little time I have to concentrate on weight loss since giving birth to my second child.

The answers in the example are made up and are just there to show you how to use this tool. By completing the daily logs over a week or two you should be starting to identify certain situations, people, events etc. that trigger your anxiety. What I want you to do now is to write all these things down in a long list. So your list may look something like this;

I feel anxious when…..

My Mum comes to visit.

When I worry that I may not have enough money to buy my

children everything they need.

When people look at me in the street.

When I have to eat in front of my workmates.

When I need to drive my car somewhere.

When I am alone.

When it is dark.

When I have to speak to anyone in public.

So you get the picture, your list may only be a few triggers long or it may be many triggers long. That doesn't matter. What matters now is looking at a way in which you can start to challenge the things that trigger your anxiety. That is how you can overcome it.

Challenging self and making changes

The next stage in this process is to put your list into a table like the one shown on the next page. As you can see there are 3 columns. Column 1 is where you write down what triggers your anxiety. Column 2 is where you think about what it is about this trigger that makes you feel anxious. Column 3 is where you write down what you can do to challenge and change this trigger. Column 3 cannot include avoiding situations.

Triggers. I feel anxious when….	What is it about this trigger that makes me feel anxious?	What can I do to challenge and change this?
My Mum comes to visit.	My Mum always says how messy my house is and starts to tidy up. This makes me feel lazy and worthless.	I care about what my Mum thinks so I can make my house clean and tidy before she arrives **OR** I don't really think it's any of Mum's business what my house is like, so next time she visits I am going to tell her to stop tidying up as it annoys me and makes me feel lazy and worthless.
When I worry that I may not have enough money to buy my children everything they need.	I never had much as a child and was bullied a little at school for not having the best trainers etc. the same as the other kids.	I can start to save a little money each week, as much as I can reasonably afford, so I can provide my child with what they need. I can recognise that my child is different to myself and just because I was

		bullied doesn't mean they will be too.
When people look at me in the street.	I think people are judging me for being overweight.	I can walk down a busy street and really notice how many people actually stare at me, chances are this will be none. I can lose weight.
When I have to eat in front of my work mates.	I don't like how much weight I have put on since I had my second child. I think I'm fatter than most other people I know.	I realise that it would probably be a good idea for my health to lose a few pounds and also help me feel better about myself. It's not about what my colleagues think but more how I see myself. I am going to try and lose some weight.
When I need to drive my car somewhere.		
When I am alone.		
When it is dark.		
When I have to speak to anyone in public.		

The next step is the most important and the hardest step you will have to do. It involves putting into practice the challenges and changes you wrote down in column 3. Now you don't have to do this for each trigger straight away, in fact it is probably advisable not to, as you may feel overwhelmed by so many changes. Instead pick one or two triggers you want to work on and then practice putting the changes and challenges into place for a week or so. When you begin you may not succeed entirely the first time but this is okay, just try again and again until you do. When you do succeed think about the following:

How you felt?

How proud you should be of yourself!

You didn't die!

The worst thing you imagine could have happened probably didn't happen!

And then give yourself a massive "congratulations" as you are now on your way to more easily recognising what may trigger any anxiety you have in the future. You have also learnt a method you can use to challenge yourself and change the effect these triggers have on you. Well done! This is another important part of overcoming anxiety, always acknowledge the positives and tell yourself you are succeeding when you are.

You can download the tables from this chapter for your personal use by visiting our website here:
http://www.monkseatoncounsellingandhypnotherapy.co.uk/downloads

TOOL 2
AFFIRMATIONS

An affirmation is a statement we make to ourselves; it is simply 'self-talk'. We make both negative and positive affirmations all day, every day, without even realising it. For example, if you don't do well during an exam you may think, *'I'm stupid, I'm never going to get anywhere in life'*. This is a negative affirmation. Or if you say to yourself, *'It's ok, I tried my best and I can re-take the exam'*, this is a positive affirmation. These affirmations we say to ourselves can dramatically impact upon our lives, affecting our self-esteem and confidence and generally influencing how we see ourselves in the world. By being aware of and changing our affirmations we can shape our thoughts and therefore change how we view ourselves resulting in higher self-esteem and increased confidence. The effects can be dramatic, we can suddenly gain the confidence and drive to do what we want in life, not letting anything hold us back.

Throughout my work, I have noticed that people who suffer from anxiety often have lots of negative affirmations that they are not even aware of. For example, someone who has an anxiety attack may tell himself, *'this is it, I'm never going to get any better'*, *'I can't breathe, I'm stupid'*, *'I must be crazy, this doesn't happen to normal people'* and so on. What we need to do is to change these negative affirmations into positive affirmations. This will help us to come out of an anxiety attack quicker and, if used regularly, may help prevent anxiety attacks all together. What you are doing is reprogramming your subconscious mind to really believe the positive affirmations and therefore making you feel better about yourself.

I have developed a 3 step guide to writing your affirmations which will allow you to gain the maximum benefit from them.

Go to our website here: http://www.monkseatoncounsellingandhypnotherapy.co.uk/downloads and download the worksheets for Tool 2. Here you will find the tables you need to complete the following 3 steps.

Step 1.

Write a list of negative affirmations you often say to yourself. These don't have to be when you are having an anxiety attack. They can be just general day to day stuff. I have included a table on the next page which shows you some examples of negative affirmations people often say to themselves. You should write your own list in the first column, negative affirmations.

Negative Affirmation	Positive Affirmation
I feel like I am stupid	I am an intelligent wo/man
I will never get anywhere in life	I am beginning to achieve what I want in life
I am really fat and ugly	I am losing weight and looking good

Step 2.

Now I want you to write a sentence in the column, positive affirmations, which turns your negative affirmation into a positive one. I have included a few examples in the table above. This may be difficult to do at first as you will not be used to saying nice positive things about yourself, but if you stick with it you will do it in time. Maybe just change one affirmation per day or per week, whatever feels okay for you. Always write your positive affirmations in the present tense, for example, instead of saying to yourself, *'I will be successful'*, say *'I am successful'*.

The Importance of Belief

In order for your affirmations to be effective you must believe them. If you don't believe what you are writing go back and start again, write something which feels more comfortable, you can change these as your confidence develops and you start to believe more in yourself. Write down your affirmations and 'own' the feelings you put in them, believe how great you are. Put your feelings into your affirmations, feel what you are writing, this way you'll feel even better about yourself.

Step 3.

In the table on the next page write down all your positive affirmations as you do them. There must be **NO** negative affirmations on here. What you must do with this list is to keep adding to it as you develop your positive affirmations and wipe out your negative affirmations. I want you to read this list out loud to yourself, or say it in your head if you prefer, each morning when you get out of bed and each night before you go to bed. Notice how this makes you feel. It is very important to do this, as this is how you reprogram your subconscious into believing the positive affirmations. If you are out in public and you feel anxious just feel the list in your pocket and remind yourself of all the good things there are about you. Maybe read this list quietly to yourself in a quiet area, re-affirming all your positive qualities to yourself. This will help you to get through any difficult situations throughout your day.

My Affirmations

1. I am an intelligent wo/man.

2. I am beginning to achieve what I want in life.

3. I am losing weight and looking good.

4. ....
....

5. ....
....

6. ....
....

7. ....
....

8. ....
....

9. ....
....

TOOL 3
FOCUSED BREATHING

This chapter on Focused Breathing, is written in partnership between myself and Jan Albertsen. Jan Albertsen is a qualified and BACP accredited Counsellor, Hypnotherapist and EFT practitioner (Level 2).

By learning to focus on and control our breathing we can help to prevent the buildup of stress and anxiety.

"If your breathing is in any way restricted, to that degree

so is your life"

~ Michael Grant White

How often do you think about your breathing? Most people do not take enough time out to concentrate on their breathing. It maintains our basic life functions, and supplies instant oxygen to all of our body cells through our bloodstream. Each breath we take nourishes our entire being. Yet most people do not spend time ensuring they breathe correctly. Breathing correctly can alleviate so much of the tension, stress, anxiety and any other symptoms which have built up over time through shallow breathing. Deep breathing takes even more oxygen to our body cells, aiding healing, by promoting a 'relaxation response' in the body, known as the parasympathetic nervous system.

On the following pages, Jan Albertsen has provided us with two breathing exercises, which he often uses in his work to help clients relax. Both of these techniques are about breathing deeply and using your breath to relax your body. The idea is that once your body is relaxed your feelings and your mind can follow, thus alleviating any tensions in the mind or body that may be causing you to feel anxious.

If at any point you start to feel dizzy simply stop the exercise until you feel okay again. Dizziness is something that can happen when we are first practicing the breathing techniques. Just give yourself time and space to find your own way with the techniques.

Audio copies of these breathing exercises, accompanied by soothing and relaxing music, are available to buy for a small fee on our website:

http://monkseatoncounsellingandhypnotherapy.co.uk/shop/

Exercise One

Relaxed Breathing

By Jan Albertsen

Start by finding somewhere quiet and peaceful. Take a few minutes to make sure you will be warm, maybe play some soft and relaxing music, have a drink to hand in case you need one and make yourself comfortable by removing any tight clothing. This is a simple way of relaxing your breathing and teaching your body to relax. It often helps people who are having trouble sleeping.

1. Lie on the floor or on a bed with your head on a cushion. Make yourself comfortable and relax your body. Lay your arms by your side and your legs can either be straight or bent at the knees. Close your eyes.

2. Place one hand on your chest and the other on your stomach. Rest them gently on your body, palm downwards.

3. Take a nice long slow breath inwards and feel your hands. The hand placed on your chest should not move, but the one placed on your stomach should rise.

4. If the hand on your chest is rising, slow you're breathing down and visualise the air flowing down into your stomach. Focus on the feeling of the air flowing down from your nose and mouth into your airways, deep down into your lungs.

5. Hold your breath for a second and then breathe out just as slowly as you breathed inwards.

6. Remember.....breathe in and stomach rises.....breathe out and stomach lowers. Take slow and easy breaths.

7. Imagine you are breathing in cool fresh air and breathing out your troubles and anxiety.

Try to do this exercise for 10 to 15 minutes at a time, but even a couple of minutes can help. During the day try to be aware of your breathing, and find your own rhythm of relaxed breathing. Once you have done this, you can use your own relaxed breathing anytime you need to calm yourself down. You can even do it in a sitting position at school or work to help you to re-focus or de-stress.

Exercise 2 follows on the next page.

EXERCISE 2

7-11 breathing

By Jan Albertsen

This is something you can use anytime anywhere, sitting in your car or on the bus, at work, or while walking down the street. If the 'in breath' or the 'out breath' feel too much try counting 6 and 10 or 5 and 9. This will make sense once you read the instructions below. The important thing is to breathe out for 3-4 seconds longer than breathing in.

1. Close your mouth and breathe in gently through your nose to the count of seven. You are breathing in slowly.

2. Feel your stomach rise.

3. Hold your breath for a second and then gently breathe out through your mouth to the count of eleven. So you are breathing out really slowly.

4. Notice how your shoulders come down as you breathe out. Feel your upper body relax. Your stomach flattens as you let all the air out of your lungs.

5. Feel the relaxation in your body.

6. Repeat this two or three times.

You can use 7-11 breathing in three different ways;

1. To reduce your anxiety when it is high.
2. To prepare yourself for a potentially anxious situation.
3. To reduce your general anxiety levels during the day.

It is really useful to practice 7-11 breathing regularly during the day, maybe every time you make a hot drink or sit down somewhere. Then your body starts to become used to a more relaxed state and, if anxiety levels do rise, using the technique will have a more powerful relaxing effect.

TOOL 4
EMOTIONAL FREEDOM TECHNIQUE (EFT)

This chapter on EFT, known as Emotional Freedom Technique is written in partnership between myself and Jan Albertsen.

EFT is a pioneering method of therapeutic healing. Many practitioners worldwide use EFT in their work, including counsellors, psychotherapists, hypnotherapists, mental health nurses and social workers. EFT is an effective therapy for both physical and emotional distress, but for the purpose of this book we will concentrate on its uses with anxiety.

"Even though EFT violates just about every conventional belief out there, the results remain remarkable. EFT isn't perfect of course. We don't get 100%. But it usually works well and the results are sometimes spectacular. It often works where nothing else will. We are still learning why EFT works so well. It centers around the profound effects of the body's subtle energy's using the theory that, the cause of all negative emotions is a disruption in the body's energy system. Accordingly, EFT is an emotional form of acupuncture except that we don't use needles.

Instead we tap with the finger tips to stimulate certain meridian energy points while the client is "tuned in" to the problem."

Gary Craig, developer of EFT.

EFT is very simple to learn, easy to use and is effective in minutes. You can do it anywhere, even whilst out shopping or having a meal. Once you notice EFT working to reduce or even eliminate your anxiety you can then use it on many different issues, such as: fears (public speaking etc.), stress, physical pain, OCD, self-esteem issues, weight loss and anger management. You simply just change the words in the different stages outlined on the following pages.

EFT is an emotional type of acupuncture, minus any needles! It works by stimulating various acupressure points to balance the natural elements in our bodies. It is done by tapping on various meridian points in sequence using your fingertips. Meridian points when stimulated cause energy shifts and balance out our emotions. This may sound a little strange but, honestly, I urge you to give it a go. The results seen with many people worldwide have been astounding.

It is advisable to be aware that it may take you a few practices to get it right, so if it does not work first time, don't give up. Try it for a few days or so and you'll soon notice a difference.

What follows is a step by step guide to using EFT with anxiety. If you find the instructions difficult to follow you can view a video tutorial on our website:

http://monkseatoncounsellingandhypnotherapy.co.uk/video-tutorials

We have made this short video as we understand that some people get confused by the steps and are sometimes not sure if they are doing it correctly.

Using EFT for anxiety

By Jan Albertsen

3 Stages of EFT:

1. Awareness. To destroy the negative imbalance which is anxiety you first need to bring it into your awareness. You just need to think about it to do this. Of course, you can practice EFT whenever anxiety arises and is already in your awareness too.
2. The next thing to do is to prepare your energy system to clear the anxiety, sometimes referred to as 'The set up'. This is done by repeating a statement to yourself out loud, for example *'Even though I feel anxious, I'm aright, I'm ok'*. You may find an alternative word or phrase to 'anxious' works better for you, if so use that. You need to say this statement to yourself about 3 or 4 four times whilst tapping the karate chop point, 'the set-up'. Tap this point vigorously with the fingertips of the index and middle finger of the other hand.
3. Follow steps 1 to 8 by tapping those points using the fingertips of the index and middle fingers. Steps 1 to 8 are the clearing process. During the clearing process you need to keep your anxiety in your awareness by repeating the set up phrase as you are tapping. Repeat the phrase once or twice while you tap each point. This reminds your body it is anxiety that you are working on.

Points to remember
1. Tap hard but don't hurt yourself.
2. You can change sides of the body, it doesn't matter which side you tap on.
3. Tap about 7 times on each meridian point.
4. You may need to do more than one round of tapping for your anxiety to reduce or disappear. That's fine,

just repeat the round using the same statement if it still fits or another one like, *'even though I still have some of this anxiety, I'm alright, I'm ok'*, if your level of anxiety has changed.
5. It may be useful to have a score in your head out of 10 for how bad the anxiety feels before you do the EFT, with 1 being not bad at all and 10 being the worst it could ever be. Then to measure any change by scoring how you feel after you have done the EFT.

Step by step guide

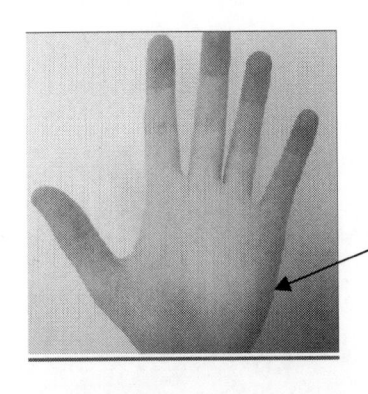

The Set-up

This meridian point is known as the 'karate chop point'. It is the fleshy part of your hand. Say the statement, 'Even though I feel anxious, I'm alright, I'm ok' out loud 3 or 4 times. Tap vigorously.

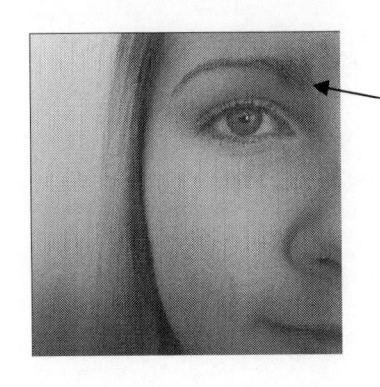

Step 1

Tap the end of your eye brow, the bit where it meets the end of your nose. Say the set up statement once or twice out loud.

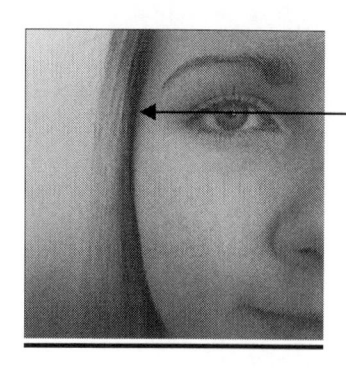

Step 2

Tap the side of the eye, where the bone is at the outer edge of the eye. Say the set up statement once or twice out loud.

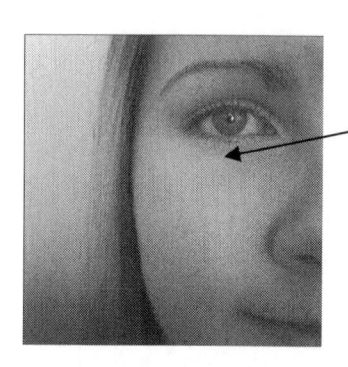

Step 3

Tap directly below the eye, in the centre on the bone of the eye socket. Say the set up statement once or twice out loud.

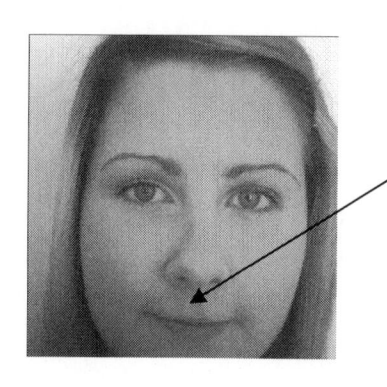

Step 4

Tap under the nose and above the lip. Say the set up statement once or twice out loud.

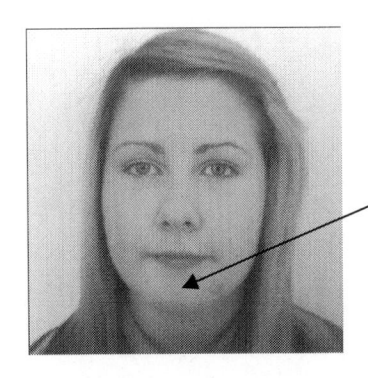

Step 5

Tap under the lower lip and above the chin. Say the set up statement once or twice out loud.

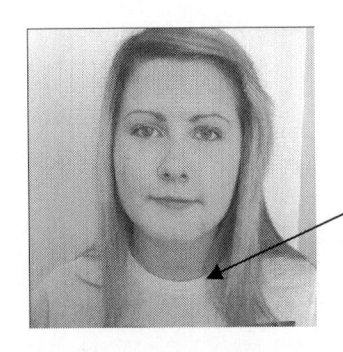

Step 6

Tap at the end of your collar bone, the bit where the bone meets the sternum. Say the set up statement once or twice out loud.

Step 7

Tap under the arm. If you are a man, tap in line with the nipple. If you are a woman, tap on the bra strap. Say the set up statement once or twice out loud.

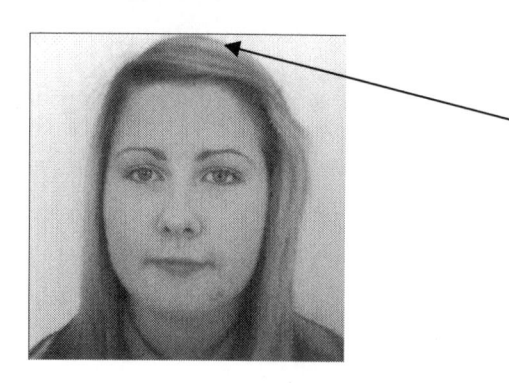

Step 8

Tap on the top of your head, at the crown. Say the set up statement once or twice out loud.

TOOL 5
DISTRACTION METHODS

Distraction methods are things we can do to take our minds away from what we are thinking and feeling. These are particularly helpful if you are not having an anxiety attack as such, but are feeling slightly anxious and feel like more serious and distressing anxiety feelings may be surfacing. The method I use is to create 'a box'. This will be known as your distraction box. You then fill this box with things that will effectively distract you. You can do this by following the steps below.

Step 1.

Begin by preparing your distraction box. You will need to find an empty box at least the size of a shoe box, bigger if you like. You can either leave this as it is, but some people I have worked with like to decorate the box and make it personal to them. This is particularly effective for young people and may be useful to pass onto any young people who you know who suffer from anxiety. I have seen people just paint it one colour, others cut pictures out of magazines and stick them onto the box and some people write things on the box that mean something to them. It is about creating a box that feels personal and best for you. It is important that you feel comfortable with it, as its purpose is to bring you calmness and distraction from anxiety.

Step 2.

When you have created your box I want you to write a list of all the things you can think of that you can put into the box which will distract you and to think about how they may do this. Your list may look something like this;

A pack of playing cards.

A photo album of people who are important to me.

Favourite music I can dance to, letting off steam.

Important item….Grandma's wedding ring I can use to focus on.

A note pad and pen so I can write my feelings down.

A drawing pad and pencils I can use to draw how I feel and let emotions out.

An electronic hand held game.

A bar of chocolate to give me a boost.

A list of my positive affirmations.

An emergency contact number of someone I can phone to talk to in case I feel the worst I can feel.

Of course, your list may be very different to this but it may also be similar, that's okay. What is important is that you have at least 5 to 8 items you can put into your distraction box.

Step 3

Gather the items in your list and put them into your box. Arrange them in whatever way feels comfortable for you.

That is it, you have now created your very own unique distraction box. What is particularly good about this distraction box is that it is personal to you. You have created a box full of items which will help to distract you from your anxiety, making you feel less anxious. If you live with others you may want to put this box away in a safe place so its contents can't be removed or damaged. You can also take it with you when you go on holiday and it will be there to hand should you need it. So next time you feel anxious, simply get out your box and open it up. Choose an item which fits your mood and use it to distract yourself from what you are feeling. Keep doing this until your anxiety subsides.

TOOL 6
SELF-CARE
SELF-MASSAGE, DIET AND EXERCISE

Self-massage

Massage is an excellent way to relieve stress, anxiety and many other negative feelings. It is widely believed, more so in the eastern world, that we can hold feelings in our bodies. These feelings can become trapped and cause all kinds of ill health, including anxiety. Many people believe that as we massage our bodies, feelings that have become trapped are stimulated and released from our bodies. One of the main aims of massage is to 'release tension'. Massage is an excellent way to release built up tension from the body, but also can do the same with many other feelings, including anxiety.

It is ideal if you have someone at home who can massage your body for you. This will help to release anxiety from the body. It will also improve your relationship with this person as you grow closer and more in tune with each other's bodies. You may want to invest in a massage guide book or borrow one from your local library to assist with correct and safe techniques. Just guide your massage partner by telling them which parts of your body feel tense and ask for that area to be massaged. Remember feelings can be held in our tension and once this tension is released so too are these negative feelings.

For the purpose of this book, I am going to focus on the use of self-massage and Indian head massage in particular to help relieve anxiety. This is for two reasons. One, I believe that massage should be available 24 hours a day and who better to do this than you? You can find a quiet area at work or whilst out shopping, anywhere in fact and do this. Two, I have been trained in the application of Indian head massage and truly believe this is one of the most effective ways to relieve tensions and anxiety from the body. However, I cannot be held responsible for the outcome of this massage. Please take care and just massage to a degree that feels comfortable. Massage should not hurt. There should be no negative side effects from Indian head massage. You may feel slightly tired just after the massage and so it is recommended to drink some water and sit still for a few minutes before going about your daily routine again.

About Indian head massage

Indian head massage has been used for thousands of years as part of traditional Indian techniques for relaxation and healing. It is an alternative treatment, used to manipulate energy channels in the shoulders, neck, head, face and ears to unblock these energy channels and expel any negative trapped energy which can cause ill health. Indian head massage works by helping to get rid of knots of tension in the neck, shoulder and facial area. The scalp is then stimulated helping to reduce and expel any build-up of tension in the head

What are the benefits of Indian head massage?

- Relieves stress and anxiety.
- Aids relaxation.
- Relieves tension.
- Expels negative energy from the body.
- Relieves headaches and migraine.
- Reduces insomnia.
- Relieves sinusitis.
- Improves blood circulation.
- Relieves neck and back pain.
- Stimulates lymphatic drainage which helps to remove toxins from the body and boost the immune system.
- Strengthens hair roots which can reduce and stop hair loss, and in some cases can even restore hair growth.

As you can see from this list there are so many health benefits to Indian head massage. It should now be obvious that it can help to relieve anxiety as it helps to reduce stresses and expel negative energy from the body, whilst promoting a more general sense of well-being. If used regularly it can be used to prevent anxiety, and can also be used when you feel anxious to help alleviate the feelings you have.

I have provided you with a guide over the next few pages which you should follow. The guide shows you were to place your hands on your body. We have also created a short video tutorial that you can watch on our website:

http://monkseatoncounsellingandhypnotherapy.co.uk/video-tutorials/

Remember…..

- You can do the following steps in any order, just do what feels best for you.

- Remove tight clothing and loosen shirt buttons before beginning, making yourself as comfortable as possible. You may even want to remove your shoes.
- Remove any headwear, slides, hair bands, etc.
- Warm your hands before the massage.
- You can apply a little oil or talc to your hands before the massage which will aid stimulation to the scalp and help the hands slide more easily through the hair.
- Have a drink of water with you for after the massage.
- You can also do this massage on others or ask them to massage you too.
- Always stop the massage if you start to feel dizzy or you feel like it is hurting you. Indian head massage should make you feel better and should not hurt.

Step by step guide to Indian head massage

Step 1 – Neck stretching

Place a hand on your left shoulder close to your neck and begin by stretching the neck slightly to the right. Neck stretching allows the muscles to begin to gently relax. Do this movement a few times and then swap and stretch the other side of the neck. You can then continue the stretching a few times on each side, stretching in clockwise and then anti clockwise directions. The purpose of neck stretching is to activate the adjacent glands and lymph nodes. This technique needs to be done very slowly and carefully and should feel comfortable. If it makes you feel dizzy then you should stop.

Step 2 – Shoulder squeezing

Place your left hand on your right shoulder quite near your neck. Squeeze the muscle between your palm and your fingers, gradually moving along the shoulder, ensuring you massage the whole shoulder area. Then repeat on your left shoulder using your right hand. This is a great method to expel stress and tension from the shoulder area. Do this 3 times on each side.

Step 3 - Neck massage

Start on one side of the neck and use the tips of your fingers to make small circles and massage just below your collar line on the back of your shoulders. Continue these circular movements up either side of the spine until you reach your hairline. Repeat this 2 more times and then swap and massage the opposite side of your neck.

Step 4 – Neck squeezing

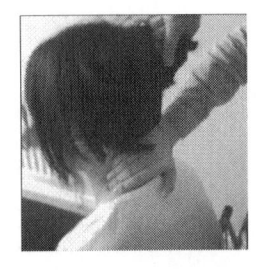

Place any hand on the back of your neck and gently squeeze between your palm and fingers. Take care not to apply direct pressure to the spine, rather concentrate on the muscles on each side of the neck. This stroke helps to improve blood circulation in the brain.

Step 5 – Scalp massage

1. Massage the head with both of your whole hands, keeping your fingertips and palms on the scalp. You should massage as if you are shampooing your hair and you can feel your scalp moving below your hands. Do this until you have covered the whole scalp.

2. Place the heel of your hand on the back of the head and rub quite vigorously back and forth rubbing as much of the scalp as you can reach. Swap hands and massage the other side of the head too.

3. Hair pulling. This should be gentle pulls on the hair. It also helps to stimulate hair growth. Gently slide your fingers through your hair until you grasp the hair between your fingers slightly away from the scalp. Pull the hair gently in the direction of hair growth then allow your hands to slip easily along the length of your hair and away from your head. Repeat this until you have covered the whole head.

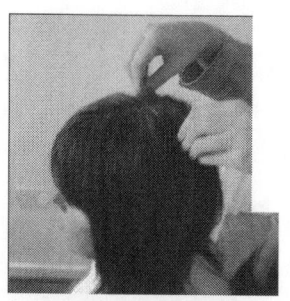

4. Hair plucking. Gently pluck at your head using your fingertips in the same way you would imagine a bird pecking at your head. Cover the whole head area.

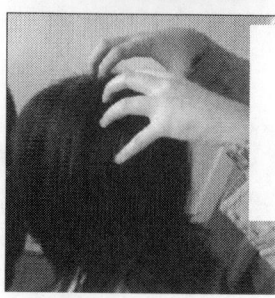

5. Tapping the head. Using your fingertips make gentle taps across the entire surface of your head, as if you were playing the piano.

6. Stimulating the nerves. Gently place your hands at the back of your head and run your fingers through your hair forward to the forehead. Then gently slide your hands back down to the base of the hairline. Repeat this until you have covered the whole head.

Step 6 – Forehead massage

Place your hands on your forehead so your fingers meet in the middle above your eyebrows. Draw your fingers out towards your temples and when you reach the temple gently rub in circles a few times with your index and middle fingers. Repeat this 2 or 3 times.

Step 7 – Eyebrow pinching

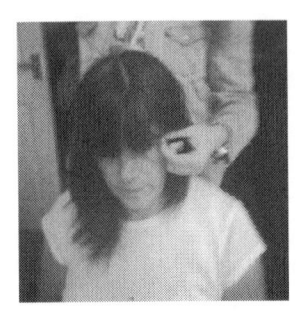

Start between the eyebrows and gently rub your middle finger along the length of the eyebrow using a moderate pressure. Repeat 3 times. Then start again between the eyebrows and pinch the eyebrow together, working your way along the whole length of the eyebrow. Repeat 3 times.

Step 8 – Ear massage

Ear massage is very calming and is known to reduce hyperactivity in children. Firstly, you simply pull the ear from the top and then release, do this 3 times. Repeat this on the back and lower ear lobe. Secondly, take your thumb and finger and pinch all around the ear. Do this 2 or 3 times. Lastly, use your middle fingers to rub around the bone at the back of the ear in small circular movements from the bottom of the ear to the top. Repeat this 2 or 3 times.

Step 9 – Finishing

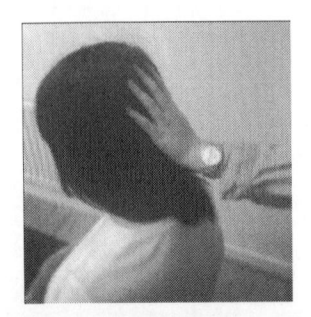

Finish the massage by gently stroking your hair from the top of your head to the end of your hair. Stop when it feels right to do so.

I learnt these methods of Indian head massage approximately 10 years ago and always practice Indian head massage this way. You will find that different schools teach it in slightly different ways, but the basics should remain the same. If you find you enjoy some areas of the massage more than others then just focus on those that benefit you the most.

Diet

Food supplies our brain and our bodies with the nutrients, vitamins and minerals we need to feel healthy!

Do you ever really take time out and think about what you are eating on a daily basis? Have you ever kept a diary about your food intake and then looked at this to see if it has any relation to the anxiety you are experiencing? I can guess that you do think about what you are eating in some way or another, we always have to think about our next meal, but what I mean is to think about certain types of foods and the impact they can have on anxiety. For example, a lot of people will feel anxious on a Sunday after they have eaten a big roast dinner. This happens as the body fights to digest all the dense carbohydrate it has just consumed, making you want to go to sleep so the body can shut down and start the digestion process. These feelings can make you feel anxious as they cause an imbalance within the body as it struggles to cope with this process. It can also make you feel breathless and 'too full' which again causes some people to feel anxious. This same principle also applies when we consume any large amount of dense carbohydrates such as bread and pasta based meals. You may also feel anxious on a Saturday or Sunday morning after heavy drinking the night before. You feel rotten after a night out drinking as you have literally poisoned your body and it needs to work hard to remove the alcohol from it. That said, most things are ok for us in moderation, drinking while eating a small dinner with plenty of green vegetables would probably leave you feeling okay, as would limiting what you drink to just one or two glasses of alcohol. You can see from this that there is a picture building about how what we put into our bodies makes us feel a certain way.

To really focus on how the foods you are consuming are affecting your anxiety you will need to fill out a table, like the one below. You can download a copy of the table from our website: http://monkseatoncounsellingandhypnotherapy.co.uk/downloads

This table will allow you to see if there are any links between what you eat and how you feel. Fill the table in for a couple of weeks and see what food makes you feel anxious; this may be apparent in one week. For example, if you feel anxious after your morning cup of coffee, then maybe this is causing you some anxiety, try cutting this cup of coffee out and see what happens. This may be your body's way of telling you that it doesn't like caffeine on an empty stomach and maybe try some decaf instead or a herbal drink. Try this for anything else you may think is causing anxiety and make a note of any changes in your anxiety levels you feel after eliminating the food or drink.

	Mon	Tue	Wed	Thur	Fri	Sat	Sun
Breakfast							
Lunch							
Dinner							
Snacks and drinks							

How did you feel after each meal/snack/drink?						

I want to focus on your diet because it can have a great influence on how you feel. What we eat really can ward off or cause anxiety. When I talk about diet, I don't mean this in terms of 'dieting', but more about overall diet and the foods we consume. What I want to share with you are some of the interesting things I have learned about food and how it can affect our mood. I do not claim to be a professional in this subject, but I do have some nutrition and health training at Degree level and have done much research in this area.

I will start by talking about foods that we should think about avoiding or limiting and the reasons why. I'll then move onto what foods we should eat and why.

What foods should we limit or avoid?

You may or may not have heard some interesting facts about red meat, dairy products and caffeine. These are the three food groups which I recommend you look at closely.

Red meat

Red meat can be particularly bad for us, and leave us feeling sluggish and heavy after we have eaten it. This is because it takes so long to digest. The fact that we have to cook it so much before we eat it means we are not naturally meant to eat it as we are fruit for example, which we can pick and consume instantly. We do not have the teeth to consume it raw or the digestive system to cope with it. In fact, eating it raw would probably make you very ill. Red meat takes about 30 hours to pass through our system, resulting in tiredness and even anxiety, as our bodies work really hard to digest it.

Dairy products

There has been an awful lot of debate about the effect of dairy products, particularly milk, on our health. Some people believe this is nonsense whilst others recommend avoiding milk at all cost, claiming it is not normal to consume something meant for calves!

To demonstrate how consuming dairy can affect how we feel I will tell you about a close friend of mine. My friend had suffered from migraines for as long as she could remember. She would have a migraine almost weekly, sometimes even more than once a week. These migraines were so severe to the point where she could not get out of bed, would vomit and be in so much pain. She had always been told and assumed these were related to her monthly cycle. As you can imagine, this caused my friend a lot of stress and she would worry about her sickness record at work, cancelling events etc. and feeling anxious about committing herself to any plans. One day I went round to her house for a cup of tea and a chat and instead of having a cup of tea she poured herself a glass of milk. I asked her why she was doing that and she said that she had a glass of milk a day. She always had since she was a child and was told you need it to make your bones strong and she had then just kept on drinking it. Immediately I knew that this may be what was causing her to have migraines and I told her how bad dairy can be for the body. She said she had heard about this before, but had never believed it and had just kept drinking her glass of milk a day. With some persuasion from myself and her husband she agreed to go cold turkey and cut milk out of her diet. The result? Her migraines stopped that day and two years later they have not returned!

This story shows just how much certain foods can affect how we feel and the quality of life we have. You may be surprised at how much effect the foods you eat are having on your life. This is because the food we eat influences how we are on the inside. You will have heard the famous saying, 'you are what you eat', well this is so true. If you eat a healthy, well balanced diet then your body and in turn your mind, will feel healthy and well balanced too. If you eat a lot of junk food and unhealthy food then you will most likely feel like junk and unhealthy too. It just makes sense to eat well.

Of course, there are many people who will say it is nonsense to avoid dairy and that it has lot of health benefits such as providing us with calcium and preventing osteoporosis, and providing us with the much needed Vitamin D, magnesium and protein we need in our diets. There have even been studies done which claim to have shown that dairy can be good for the heart and can lower blood pressure. However, on the other hand it is also known that it is harmful for babies under one to drink milk as it can cause iron deficiency and there is much controversy about the contaminants found in milk such as pesticides which can be harmful to the body over time. I've mentioned the possible benefits here about dairy too as I believe that everyone should make an informed choice and because it causes much debate.

Caffeine

Caffeine is a natural stimulant which is well known to make people feel anxious, nervous and sometimes paranoid. It a drug that affects our brain. I cannot drink coffee at all and not because I don't like it, I love it! But it causes me to have heart palpitations and feel quite ill so I avoid it at all costs. Caffeine can also disturb sleep and it is well known that tiredness causes anxiety. Tea, fizzy pop, energy drinks and chocolate also contain caffeine.

There are also some other foods which it is advisable to learn more about if you decide to look at how your diet can influence how anxious you feel in more depth. These include the following:

Acid forming foods

If you eat a lot of acid forming foods and your body is too acidic then this can cause you to feel anxious. Acid forming foods are fine in moderation, but can cause problems if you overdo it. Acid forming foods include protein, dairy products and processed foods. Acidic foods are known to make it hard for the body to eliminate toxins which reduces your resistance to stress and other illnesses and may also make you feel weak. All of these things can cause anxiety.

Alcohol

When you first drink alcohol you may well feel like it is relaxing you, but alcohol is a well-known depressant drug which can cause depression and anxiety. It is best not to drink at all, but if you want to, or have a special occasion coming up at which alcohol is part of the celebration, then it is best to drink in moderation. It is recommended by the UK government that adult women consume only 2-3 units of alcohol per day which is the equivalent to one 175ml glass of wine and that men should not exceed 3-4 units of alcohol per day, which is the equivalent to a pint and a half of 4% beer.

Sugar

You should avoid sugary foods in excess. Sugar causes our blood circulation speed to increase which can make us feel anxious. Sugary foods that are bad for us include; chocolate, sweets, cakes, some crisps and dressings, soft drinks and other items. Sugar is often hidden in some foods so it is best to check the label.

White foods

White foods such as white bread, white rice and white potatoes all increase our blood sugar levels which can cause us to feel anxious.

Processed foods

Some people recommend avoiding any processed foods which includes all frozen, tinned, refrigerated and dried foods. Of course, in the modern world this can be very hard to achieve. It is often not the food itself that is the problem, as scientific evidence shows that when food is frozen for example it actually retains a lot of its goodness, but it is more the chemicals that are added. These can often have harmful effects on our body, especially over time.

What foods should we eat and why?

Eating an alkaline diet

An alkaline diet means you need to consume at least 80% fruits and vegetables such as apples, pears, oranges, cucumber, broccoli, sprouts and many other fruit, vegetables, seeds and nuts. In fact, we should eat as many different kinds of fruit and vegetables as we can. They are jam packed with all the nutrients and minerals we need to maintain an optimum level of health. The other 20% can be more fruit and vegetables or acidic foods like meat. Remember this is all about balance and discovering what is best for you and your body, and finding the right balanced diet that creates harmony in your body and promotes emotional and physical balance.

Good fats

The good fats that we should eat include monounsaturated fat and polyunsaturated fat. The two fats that are bad for our health and we should avoid are saturated fat and trans fat.

Good fats are found in oily fish, seeds, nuts, flax seed oil, avocados, olive oil, canola oil, sunflower oil, peanut oil, peanut butter, sesame oil, soybean oil, corn oil, soymilk and tofu.

Fish is not only a great source of protein, it is so much easier to digest than meat and it is probably the best source of good fat you can find. Oily fish is particularly beneficial to us as it is a good source of omega 3 polyunsaturated fatty acids. These good fats are known to reduce the risk of death from heart disease, strokes and cancer. They can prevent and reduce the symptoms of depression and protect against memory loss and dementia. They are also being found to ease arthritis, joint pain, and inflammatory skin conditions and to support a healthy pregnancy. It is recommended to eat 2 portions of oily fish a week. Oily fish include salmon, trout, herring, mackerel, sardines, ell, pilchards, kipper, whitebait and fresh tuna. These fish count as oily fish when they are canned (except tuna), fresh or frozen.

Whole grains

Eating whole grains with your meal has been shown to reduce the risks of many chronic diseases such as strokes, type 2 diabetes and heart disease as well as helping with weight management.

Whole grains contain the entire grain kernel - the bran, germ, and endosperm. Whole grains include whole-wheat flour, bulgur (cracked wheat), whole cornmeal, oatmeal and brown rice.

Vitamins

It is often suggested that people who suffer from anxiety should take vitamin B as it unlocks the energy in foods. Vitamin B6, in particular, is recommended, as it is known to help the creation of serotonin in the brain. Always read the advice on any vitamin packaging and never take more than the recommended dose.

Water and hydration

It is very important to keep hydrated and most doctors will tell you that if you become dehydrated you are more likely to feel unwell, shaky and can feel anxious. Make sure you carry some water with you wherever you go and you drink enough so that you don't become very thirsty at any point. Our brain is made up of 85% water and we need to keep it hydrated to function properly.

The purpose of providing you with this detailed information is to help you become more aware of the effects some foods can have on your health. These foods do not make everyone feel the same, we all have different bodies and therefore we are all affected differently by what we eat. With some knowledge and understanding you can begin to think about your own diet and make changes to ensure you are feeling the best that you possibly can. Of course, there are lots of foods that people say are bad for us and the list changes all the time, and the effects of consuming foods differ from person to person. We get told we should not eat any meats at all, we should not drink any alcohol at all and cut out all refined sugars, harmful fats and fizzy drinks. These are what I can think of just off the top of my head. If you look online there are so many people recommending we eat this and that and don't eat this and that, that it can just become so confusing and overwhelming that we don't really know what to do for the best! I'm a great believer in everything in moderation is ok, unless of course you realise that a certain food or drink, caffeine for example, is causing you ill health, then of course it would make sense to take this out of your diet. It is all about learning what 'your' body does and does not like and eating to achieve your optimum health.

N.B. It is important to check with your health care provider before making any radical changes to your diet, especially if you have any known health condition or any unanswered questions. Also, if you feel that you cannot do this on your own then your health care provider should be able to arrange for you to see a dietician to support you. You should also tell them if you feel you have a problem with addiction, such as cigarettes or alcohol, as there are so many ways that they can work with you to help you to stop.

Exercise

It may sound dramatic but exercise really can be the miracle cure you have been looking for. It is well known that exercise reduces coronary heart disease, stroke, type 2 diabetes, colon cancer, breast cancer, early death, osteoarthritis, fractures, depression, anxiety and dementia. When we exercise we release hormones in the brain such as endorphins which improve our mood and 'burn off' stress by metabolising neurotransmitters created during the stress response. Exercise is also known to balance your blood sugar levels up to a massive 36 hours after exercise. It relaxes you by releasing muscle tension, and improves blood flow to the brain bringing with it additional needed sugars and oxygen.

Some people with anxiety believe that exercise may make them feel worse. They associate feeling breathless with anxiety and fear that this will lead to an anxiety attack. This is simply not true, exercise will only make you feel better, as long as it is done safely and within your limits.

What exercise should I do?

This depends on your current state of health. If you have not exercised for a long time and are unfit then you should not rush in and do a full 2 hour anaerobic exercise class, starting with a gentle walk will be sufficient. You can increase what you do daily as your fitness increases. Start by doing what you feel able to do. Even if this just involves running up the stairs one or two times, this is better than not running up the stairs at all. The week after you may be able to run up and down the stairs 10 times, imagine how many times you could run up and down the stairs in a few months time if you increase this daily!

There are many ways you can exercise, below is just a sample of what is available to you:

- Walking
- Running
- Skipping
- Jogging
- Trampolining
- Bike riding
- Gym classes
- Swimming
- Keep fit classes such as boxercise or aerobics
- Home exercise DVDs
- Exercise bike
- Step machine
- Games – basketball, netball, volleyball, badminton, tennis, etc.
- Martial arts
- Weightlifting (you can even use tins of baked beans!)
- Yoga

Exercising has effects on the body. When you exercise you should increases your heart rate and break into a sweat. If you can still talk whilst exercising then this type of exercise is known as moderate intensity exercise and it is recommended that a healthy adult from 19 to 64 years old should do at least 150 minutes each week. This can be broken up into 30 minute slots 5 times a week. You can also do vigorous intensity exercise which means that you would be breathing very fast and hard, your heart rate would increase substantially and it would be difficult to say more than a few words without stopping to catch your breath. It is thought that you only need to do 75 minutes of this type of exercise each week to have the same effect as 150 minutes of moderate intensity exercise. There are other types of exercise to stretch and strengthen our muscles, but to do these you should always have an induction at a gym first to ensure you are using weights and machinery correctly and you are exercising safely.

You may find that you don't like exercising alone. If this is the case then you can join a gym and ask a friend to go with you. This has extra benefits in that you will spend time with other people and build up friendships. Spending time being social also helps to reduce anxiety.

As you can see there are so many ways to exercise and a lot of these are free! There really is no excuse at all and if you say you do not have the energy to exercise well then this is just one of the worst excuses you can have, as exercising has been proven to increase your energy levels, so you really do have no excuse!

N.B. It is important to check with your health care provider before making any radical changes to your lifestyle, especially if you have any known health condition or any unanswered questions. Your GP will tell you if it is safe for you to embrace a new fitness regime and any gym should be happy to offer you an induction.

TOOL 7
DIARY AND JOURNAL WRITING

Writing about how we are feeling and what is happening in our lives has long been recognised as a healthy way to express ourselves and a way to encourage healing. It can help us to focus on areas of our lives that are important to us. It can also enable us to understand ourselves better, and to discover solutions and overcome problems we may have.

What is the difference between journalling and keeping a diary?

Firstly I would just like to say that it is worth keeping both a diary and a journal. I will explain why. A diary is like an account of events that have occurred throughout your life, it helps you to keep track of what has happened on each date and is somewhere you can easily refer back to. A diary is essentially a written record of your day, usually very factual and a great reference tool. It is only necessary to purchase a simply standard yearly diary to do this and at the end of each night just write a very brief account of what happened throughout the day.

For the purpose of this book I'd like to focus more on journalling. Journalling serves much more of a purpose than keeping a diary. A journal is a place when you can explore everything that is happening in your world and begin to make sense of yourself and your surroundings. It is more of an exploration and healing exercise than keeping a diary. A lot of people think that it will be hard work to keep a journal, well the truth is that it can be as easy or as hard as you make it! The great thing is that there are no strict rules about it, it is up to you to practice and experiment and decide what best suits your needs.

To help you understand more about journalling and how it can help you to overcome anxiety, I will answer some of the most common questions that I have been asked during my work with clients. I think this is the easiest way to explain all about it.

When should I start journalling?

There is no simple answer to this question. You can start journalling at any time in your life. Some people journal all of the time whilst others tend to dip in and out of it and only journal at certain times, such as a life crisis or significant event, taking a break and coming back to it when they need to. It is about finding a pattern that works best for you.

What should I journal in?

There are many ways to journal. Some people may purchase a simple spiral bound note pad and use this to record their day. Others may buy a large drawing pad and simply fill the journal as they wish with a series of words and drawings. Other people view journalling as a spiritual event and like a journal to match this, so they may purchase an expensive book with a soft and attractive cover, something that feels special enough to hold their inner most secrets. It really is up to you to decide what is best. Most people start with a simple spiral bound note pad and if they develop a love of journalling they buy that special book.

What are the benefits of keeping a journal?

One of the biggest benefits of keeping a journal is that you will not be judged. You can share your deepest fears, your darkest thoughts, your biggest joys, what you feel guilty about, and what you want in your life. You can cry, you can laugh, and say whatever you want and it will never tell you that what you have written is wrong or not allowed or silly or stupid, or any of the other things you are afraid someone may say to your face. It is a place where you can safely show your intimate side.

Keeping a journal can help to reduce stress and improve well-being. It is a place you can write down everything that is troubling you and get it out of your system. This helps to remove the negative feelings from your body by putting them on to paper. This often helps you to clarify what is happening and put things into a better and more positive perspective, reducing stress and improving overall well-being.

Keeping a journal can help us to focus and make plans for the future. When we write things down we get a greater sense of what it is we are actually wanting to say and what it is we want from life. Once we know these things we can then start to put plans in place to achieve them.

Keeping a journal is making time in the day just for you. In today's world we are usually so busy with our daily lives that we forget to have some 'me time' or 'time out'. We make excuses such as the washing up needs done, or we need to take the bins out, or we need to help our child with their homework, or we need to finish painting the lounge and so on. We also live in a world now where everything is done via technology and we are quickly losing the feeling of putting pen to paper and actually writing. Journalling allows us to actually sit with a pen and paper and work through our feelings. If you book a time slot in each week and dedicate this to your journal then you will find that it actually becomes an enjoyable 'task', and one you look forward to. It is also a break from all the technology in our lives, and gives us the space and time to just slow down and focus on what is really important. It can be so fulfilling and life enhancing.

What should I write about and how can journalling help me overcome anxiety?

You can write about whatever you would like to write about. There are no rules to this. Some people like to set an agenda and to write about that. For example, for the purpose of dealing with anxiety, you may find that you know what it is in your life that makes you feel anxious. So to help with this you decide that you will write each week about these things until it becomes clear why they leave you feeling anxious. Then you can write about what you can do to overcome them. If you are not sure what causes you to feel anxious you may want to just write about whatever comes into your head. This can be about anything. You may want to write about how you feel, how your day has been, who you spend time with, how work/school was, what you had for lunch, or how anxious you have felt on that day. If you do this often enough you should then come to a point where it becomes clear what is causing you to feel anxious. By looking back through your journal it may be obvious that on the days you feel anxious your Dad comes to visit, or when you have to get the bus into work instead of taking the car. The great thing about keeping a journal is that you can always refer back to how your past few days, weeks, months and even years have been, and from this you can see patterns develop. It is a great way to explore who we are and why we are the way we are. It really does give you a deep insight into yourself.

How much should I write?

Again there are no rules about this. Some people write only a few lines and this is enough for them, whilst some people may write a few pages or, if they have had a particularly good or bad day, they may write substantially more than usual. This all depends on how you feel and what has happened throughout the day. Just go with what feels natural to you and you'll soon find your own unique writing style. The important thing is that you feel a sense of achievement after you have written your journal.

How do I keep my journal safe?

A lot of people worry that when they keep a diary or a journal someone will see it and it will end up causing more problems than it solves. For people who live alone or with others who respect their privacy this is not usually a problem and you can just leave your journal in a safe place, such as your underwear drawer. However, if you don't feel confident and fear that someone will look at it, then you may need to hide it or keep it with you. However, keeping it with you means it is more likely to get lost and then be seen by others so you are best to look for somewhere at home that it will not be found, maybe under the edge of a carpet or at the back of a wardrobe. If there is something particularly sensitive to you that you'd like to write about then you could use code words in your writing. For example, if you did not want to name a person you may want to give them a code word instead. This does not even have to be another name but could just be an object. For example, your 'mother' becomes the 'tea pot' and your house becomes 'the tea room'. As long as you know what these code words mean then it makes no difference if it makes no sense to others who read it. You may also want to draw little pictures to represent how you feel or a symbol for an event. It is your journal and you can fill it how you wish.

In conclusion, keeping a journal is a way to keep focused on what is really important to you. It is something you can look back on time and time again and read about everything you have overcome. It is a place where you can instantly see how far you have developed and grown as a person. For some people it is something to leave behind for their children and grandchildren so that one day they can get to know all about you. It can be a means of ensuring that we leave behind a bit of us that we want people to know about. It is a great way of keeping our spirit alive.

TOOL 8
VISUALISATION FOR MIND RELAXATION

By Jan Albertsen

This is a visualisation which will allow you to relax. It uses the power of your mind to take you to a relaxed and safe place that you choose. A relaxing time and space would be best to do this exercise, but it is something you can use most places to help you to relax and give you a chance to recharge your mind, body and soul. Some relaxing music will help. When you first use it preferably make yourself comfortable somewhere, and allow your mind to go on a relaxing journey. You can read this exercise to yourself beforehand and become familiar with it or you can get someone you trust to read it to you. An audio copy of this visualisation, accompanied by soothing and relaxing music, is available to buy for a small fee on our website:

http://monkseatoncounsellingandhypnotherapy.co.uk/shop/

Visualisation

Start by taking a few relaxing breaths and close your eyes.

Now allow yourself to relax, more and more deeply, just allow yourself to float across time and space... your mind and imagination drifting easily...

And in a moment, allow your mind to take you to a very special place, somewhere you feel relaxed, at peace, and safe...

It may be somewhere you have visited, or somewhere you have created in your imagination...

Allow this place to come into your awareness, easily and naturally, no need to hurry, just let it float up into your awareness...

Somewhere you feel relaxed and safe, faraway from any anxiety...

Maybe it is somewhere from a holiday, somewhere close by, a place you went with somebody special, a beach, a forest, a mountain walk, a dream, floating in a magic rainbow, wherever you want it to be...

It is your choice... allow yourself that freedom... take yourself there...

And as you enter into this place give yourself a present...

Allow yourself to experience all the lovely feelings of relaxation, safety, and peace, that belong in this space, that belong to you....

See what you would see, look around you...

Hear what you would hear, listen for a moment...

Smell the smells... maybe there is a distinctive smell...

Feel the sensations on your skin, maybe the warmth of the sunshine or the coolness of the breeze...

Taste the tastes... maybe something from the air around you...

Take a deep breath, and look at everything around you, take a deep breath and breathe in the relaxation...

And feel the freedom you feel in this space, if you feel like it take a walk around, and explore your special place, or maybe you want to sit down or lie down or curl up wherever you want, or whatever you want. This place is here just for you...

And allow yourself to sense the whole experience, wherever this takes you, however you want to be there, whatever stands out most for you, allow yourself to be there...

And feel yourself absorbing this wonderful relaxed feeling. The calmness is soothing you, and a feeling of safety and peace is growing deep within you.

Allow yourself to relax in this special place, and with each breath you take the feeling of being in this place settles and calms you more and more. You can stay here as long as you wish and allow your mind, body and soul to recharge...

Feel that sense of control and peace...

And you can remain in this special place of yours for as long as you wish...

Receiving what you need...

Knowing that you can return here whenever you wish...

And when you feel ready, become aware of your surroundings, gently bringing yourself back to the here and now...

N.B. This visualisation may make you feel sleepy or even make you go to sleep.

TOOL 9
PHYSICAL RELAXATION

By Jan Albertsen

This relaxation will help you relax your whole body. It is especially useful for helping with sleep problems. Try reading though it several times and familiarising yourself with it. There is no right or wrong way to relax, it is about finding what works for you personally. You can use these words as guidance or suggestion, and feel free to adapt them to help them work for you. Give yourself at least 15 minutes to relax when you have nothing else to do. Make yourself comfortable, either sitting or lying down, and with your eyes open or closed. Remember to take your time. You can read this exercise to yourself beforehand and become familiar with it or you can get someone you trust to read it to you. An audio copy of this physical relaxation, accompanied by soothing and relaxing music, is available to buy for a small fee on our website:

http://monkseatoncounsellingandhypnotherapy.co.uk/shop/

Physical Relaxation

It is good to start by taking a few calming breaths. Feel the soothing softness of the air flowing into your lungs, letting your breath relax you...

And allow yourself to let go of any worries or anxieties, just focus on how your body feels...

From the top of your head to the tips of your toes, feel a warm flow of relaxation moving down through your body...

Notice your breathing, breathing easily, feeling yourself letting go with each breath...

Think about the top of your head to begin with, focus on your muscles below your skin and feel the tension draining away... just feel each muscle relaxing and letting go...

Feel the warm flow of the relaxation moving down from the top of your head to your forehead, allowing it to smooth out and relax... feel the relaxation flowing over your face, calming the skin and your muscles, around your eyes and your cheeks, letting them feel easy...

Smooth and easy...

And relax... with each breath you breathe feel your body becoming heavier, letting go of any tension...

Imagine yourself asleep, breathing slowly, gently, steadily and evenly...

Just enjoying that relaxed sensation, feeling any tension flowing away...

Now the rest of your face, your cheeks... muscles around your mouth and your jaw... just feel it flowing away now... let the feeling spread...

Feel the tension drifting away like smoke in the breeze...

Or feel it flowing away like water flowing down a stream...

Breathing gently and easily...

And your whole face feels relaxed now...

Feel a gentle wave of relaxation flowing over your body...

Allow the warmth to flow down into your neck and shoulders now... along to the tops of your arms... letting all tensions drain away from these areas... feel yourself sending out a wave of thought that relaxes each muscle as it goes...

... flowing down through your arms, to your elbows, through your forearms to your wrists into your hands and fingers... It feels really easy now as you are learning to let go... feel each breath...

Becoming more aware of your gentle, easy breathing...

Allowing any tension to melt away...

Feel yourself becoming stiller and quieter...

It feels easy to let go...

...just letting all those muscles be beautifully relaxed and easy... very lazy... feeling your breathing, gently and easily... more slowly, as you relax more and more... allowing your breath to breathe out any tension in your chest... letting you breathe with your stomach muscles... feeling your upper body letting go and sinking deeper into a smooth relaxed place...

Take a moment to appreciate the feeling moving, relaxing you as it moves...

Maybe you can see it as a relaxing light moving through your body...

Feel a sense of warmth flowing through your body as you relax, a sense of warmth and calmness deep down in your muscles... feeling heavy and warm...

The warmth healing and comforting as you allow your body to let go...

Sense your back now, and send a wave of warm relaxation along your back muscles, feel it moving down, maybe pausing if you feel a knot of tension and give the wave a moment to untie the tensions... and let the relaxation flow through all your back muscles... allow your breath to release any tension away...

... and your hips and thighs... feeling the natural flow of relaxation through your muscles... your body feeling heavier and more at rest with each breath...

Allowing this to flow on through your knees, down through the calves... just allowing all those areas to relax and let go, as you think about your ankles... and your feet, right the way down to the tips of your toes... feeling a blissful, peaceful feeling growing in your body and in your mind...

... feeling your breath, gentle and slow now, feeling your body relaxing more and more with each breath, allowing your mind to relax...

Breathing gently and easily...

...and when you feel ready, become aware of your surroundings, gently bringing yourself back to the here and now...

N.B. This physical relaxation may make you feel sleepy or even make you go to sleep.

TOOL 10
UNWANTED THOUGHTS
THE STOP, REWIND AND RE-PLAY METHOD

Many of the people who I have worked with over the years who have suffered from anxiety have also experienced unwanted thoughts. These thoughts can be very disturbing and can cause anxiety and panic attacks unless they are dealt with.

An unwanted thought is a thought we have in our head which may cause a range of feelings including; upset, hurt, distress, anger, fear, paranoia and worry or any other negative feelings. These feelings are closely related to those of anxiety and may cause an attack to happen. Many people have unwanted thoughts every day and simply ignore them and do not give them a second thought. For others they can be extremely distressing.

People who I have worked with in the past have had thoughts such as, *'I am such a fat cow'* and, *'I'm a terrible father I should just kill myself'*. If these thoughts take over they can lead to high levels of anxiety.

I developed my own way of working with unwanted thoughts which I call the 'stop, rewind and re-play' method.

I will use the following unwanted thought to illustrate how this works. Remember that you can use this method for as many thoughts as you want, and as many times as you want, until you feel better. The following is just an example. You should replace the example given with your own unwanted thoughts.

Example - Unwanted thought: *"I'm a terrible father, I should just kill myself."*

Step 1 – Stop button

As soon as you have an unwanted thought and it keeps occurring and will not go away, I want you to imagine you are pressing a stop button. This button can look however you want it to look. As soon as you press this button the thought will stop and it will be clear and un-threatening. The thought will still be with you, but you have stopped it and have the power to change it. It is helpful if you can say to yourself out loud, *'I have stopped this thought and I am going to make it go away'*.

So, I think to myself, *'I'm a terrible father, I should just kill myself'* (your thought here) and I have pushed the stop button and I can make this thought go away. It cannot continue without my permission!

Step 2 - Rewind button

As soon as you have stopped the thought then the next step is to rewind it in your head. This may take a little practice. People who I have worked with have told me of a few ways they have been able to do this. One person imagined a cassette tape rewinding until she was certain the thought had been rewound to just before it happened. Another person talked about how he used to say the unwanted thought backwards in his head, and another used to imagine the thought he had just before the unwanted thought. It is important that you feel that the thought is re-wound before you continue to the next step. Remember this may take some practice, but keep with it as you can make it work.

Step 3 – Re-play button

The next step is to replace, 're-play', the unwanted thought with a more positive thought. This can be any thought you like and can be related to the unwanted thought or can be entirely different. It sometimes helps to have positive thoughts written down in case you cannot think of one straight away.

The replacement thoughts may look like this.

1. *"I'm a terrible father but that doesn't mean I deserve to die."* (related to old thought)
2. *"I'm not a terrible father at all, I'm often too hard on myself."* (new thought entirely)

Say this new thought over and over to yourself until you have forgotten the unwanted thought, and are happy with the new thought. This may only take once or many repetitions. In time this method will become like second nature to you.

The reason this method works is that you are telling yourself to forget the unwanted thought, and therefore the feelings associated with it are also forgotten. You are then re-programming your brain to think a more pleasant thought and so the feelings you experience are more pleasant. This leads to less anxiety and more positive feelings.

The great thing about this method is that you can do it anywhere and no one will ever know what you are doing, unless of course you decide to say these thoughts out loud! Give it a try and keep practicing, it will work for you and lead to a more positive outlook on life.

CONCLUSION

Now that we are at the end of the book I do hope that you have found several of the tools useful, and have learnt new ways to help you to overcome your anxiety and lead a more fulfilling life. It is my hope that you are well on your way to becoming anxiety free and you can see a future in front of you where you are in control.

You may remember in the Introduction to this book that I asked you to write *'I will be ok'* on a little piece of paper and an exercise to do with this. What I want you to do now, and only if you have done this exercise, read this book fully and tried several of the tools, is to place that piece of paper in the palm of your hand and just focus on it. Think about how different you feel now compared to when you first started this book. What you have been doing is affirming to yourself that you will be ok, and it is my belief that you will be. It may take a little time, hard work and perseverance, but you will get there!

Writing this book has felt like an emotional journey for me. I have been reminded how bad my anxiety used to be and how much hard work it took me to eventually overcome it. I have shared with you the most effective ways that I have learned to overcome anxiety, and I hope you get a sense of how much I do care and how important it is to me that you gain something from this book.

I wish you every success on your journey in life.

ABOUT THE AUTHORS

Maria has been counselling children, young people and adults for the last 8 years. She is also a qualified youth and community worker. Maria has recently taken a break from counselling to concentrate on raising her two boys, age 3 and 4 years and explore other business ventures.

Qualifications

* MA in Counselling.
* Diploma in Counselling.
* BSc (Hons) Health Studies.
* Diploma in Indian Head Massage
* Certificate in Youth and Community Work.

Jan has 15 years experience as a counsellor, 6 as a hypnotherapist and 2 as an emotional freedom practitioner. He currently counsels at a young people's project and a local university as well as running his own private counselling and hypnotherapy practice.

Accreditation and professional body membership.

Jan is an accredited member of the British Association for Counselling and Psychotherapy (BACP). He adheres to the BACP Ethical Framework for Good Practice in Counselling and Psychotherapy.

Qualifications

* MA in Counselling.
* Diploma in Hypnotherapy.
* Level 2 Certificate in EFT.

CONNECT WITH US

www.theanxietysuffererstoolbook.co.uk (The Unlimited Edition)

www.mariaalbertsen.co.uk

www.monkseatoncounsellingandhypnotherapy.co.uk

www.counsellingonlineuk.co.uk

Facebook: www.facebook.com/mariaalbertsen.co.uk

Twitter: @MariaAlbertsen_

Printed in Great Britain
by Amazon.co.uk, Ltd.,
Marston Gate.